WEATHERED STEAM LOCOMOTIVES

A Modellers Guide to Prototype Weathering

by Andy J.Small

BOOK LAW PUBLICATIONS

Copyright Book Law Publications 2011
ISBN 978-1-907094-42-2

Weathering, we are off to Weathering! Actually this Thompson B1 was off to Derby and was just heading away from Heeley station with a local from Sheffield in January 1964. This particular picture illustrates the extremes of weathering experienced by the 12 inches to the Foot railway. The smokebox could be regarded as newly painted and as we progress rearwards along the boiler the weathering is at first applied gently for the first few feet and then it gets heavier until! It existed and if we want to copy the prototype railways then we too have to go to extremes too - but that is a personal, and sometimes bold choice. Even the passenger rolling stock is weathered and that was usually sent through washing plants!

Printed and bound by The Amadeus Press, Cleckheaton, West Yorkshire
First published in the United Kingdom by Book Law Publications, 382 Carlton Hill, Nottingham, NG4 1JA

CONTENTS

Foreword

A vast amount has been written over the last few years with regard to weathering and detailing ready-to-run locomotives and rolling stock. Some manufacturers now release most new locomotives in a choice of either "Pristine" or "Weathered" finishes, such is the popularity and interest of the subject.

Understandably many modellers are hesitant to take paint and/or other applications to "mucky up" their recent purchase, many of which nowadays cost in excess of £100, in case it all goes wrong. However, several companies and cottage industries have emerged which, for a fee, will perform this task for you and, to their credit, some of the results are stunning.

During the last two decades of steam motive power on British Railways, cleaning and maintenance became a low priority as engine shed staff became difficult to recruit. Better paid jobs were becoming increasingly available without the unsocial hours endured by motive power staff; after life in the engine shed environment, cleaner working conditions were not difficult to find outside the railways. BR was already committed to dieselisation, even though steam locomotives were still being built, but by 1965 major overhauls for the latter were extremely rare. Although shed staff tried their best, and indeed top-link passenger locomotives (especially on the Western Region) had the odd oily rag across them, the majority of steam locomotives became increasingly decrepit (the diesel fleet did not fare much better having to share the same personnel problems as the steam fleet).

Of course, they were not all filthy, just most of them. Occasionally clean locomotives did show-up, usually ex-works and sometimes the engine shed cleaners had a chance of honing their skills. This book gives a cross sectional aspect of the fleet in the decade from 1957 to 1964. Apparently there was a group of enthusiasts in the late Sixties' who travelled around the country visiting various engine sheds and, with permission, "bulled up" various locomotives which were diagrammed for work the next day. They were then able to photograph a relatively clean locomotive at their choice of location – what dedication!

The one common factor in all the information and "How to Guides" is that a photograph of the subject you are attempting to create is vital. This book is unashamedly designed to assist in doing just that, depicting steam locomotives within their latter 10 years of service in a work stained state.

The book is set out in sections with the British Railways Standards classes getting their contribution in followed by the locomotives inherited from the old Big Four companies by BR. Due to the excellent subject material available via the late Keith Pirt, the Eastern Region photographs outnumber the others, but this is not a personal preference and I hope in no way detracts from the subject itself.

If you are attempting to weather a locomotive for the first time, a good idea is to practise on an old model or a spare locomotive body – perhaps purchased at a swap meet or second hand stall – in that way your technique can be perfected and you can see what works best for you.

So go on - have a go. Just remember, less is more!

Andy.J.Small, Newcastle-under-Lyme, August 2011.

Working an Up empty cement train, BR Standard 9F No.92142 lays a smokescreen across Ordsall, south of Retford, in October 1961. This particular New England based 2-10-0 was only just over four years old at the time. It was withdrawn, surplus to requirements, in February 1965. Reproducing this type of weathering takes patience, and some skill, but is worth the effort if you want that prototypical finish and you run New England 9Fs on your layout.

(left) One of my favourite steam locomotives. These hard working types were very rarely kept clean and here is a prime example. The buffer beam red has been obliterated in places and the ash from the smokebox has been allowed to accumulate around the door and running plate.

(below) The boiler and cylinders are covered in a rusty brown shade which has completely blotted out the once black livery.

Some eighteen months earlier, another New England '9' No.92149, also pushing out a fine exhaust, passes Ordsall with an Up heavy freight in lovely spring light during March 1960. Again the NWE (New England) finish is quite heavy but it was real.

Smoke deflectors, smokebox, and the whole boiler all covered in road dirt, dust, ash and grime.

The buffer beam red has been replaced with a grimy black and the middle lamp has also nearly blended in.

Some seven years on, in March 1967, one of the surviving 9Fs, Birkenhead's No.92166, prepares to depart from Neville Hill yard with an empty oil tank block train destined for Stanlow oil refinery in Cheshire. Note the virtual uniform staining on the oil tanks.

The overhead electrification warning flash and the patch of rust offer a little relief from the overall dark greasy appearance.

This locomotive is dirtier than the oil tanks it is in charge of! If there was ever a crest on the tender side it has long succumbed to the inevitable. The cab side number could also claim to be a spotter's nightmare.

Kingmoor 'Britannia' No.70007 COUER-DE-LION makes a smokey departure south from Perth with a very short train of brake vans in September 1964. This Class 7 was destined to be the first to be condemned and cut up, an event which took place in June 1965 whilst it was in for overhaul at Crewe works. The contrast between the external condition of the brake vans and the locomotive is quite striking.

(Above) Rust around the running plate and cylinder forms the only break to the overall drab black appearance.

(Right) A light load indeed for a once proud class of express passenger locomotives. The nameplate is just legible amongst the dirt, who would believe this engine was once green.

Still hauling the top link expresses where they could find the work – just – and usually, at this time, as stand-ins for failed diesels, the Britannia Pacifics could still present a pleasant appearance depending on where they were allocated. Longsight's No.70016 ARIEL stands at Llandudno Junction shed under a dark threatening sky in June 1962.

The oily motion of this locomotive is in places a light brown, about the same colour as clean engine oil. A thin coat of satin varnish over a thin wash of the correct shade should achieve this appearance.

(right) Dusty but tidy, someone, perhaps a cleaner at the Manchester depot, has left contrasting shiny sections on the door.

Crewe North's No.70051 FIRTH OF FORTH heads a southbound local train from Birmingham to Bristol near Standish Junction in June 1963. The emphasis at 5A by now was to keep the motive power going; cleaning had taken a back seat – forever.

One of the former Polmadie 'Brits' with high sided tenders, its livery, which can just be made out, is Brunswick green. The water stains along the boiler top are plainly visible, again a light load for a crack West Coast Main Line express type.

The smoke box door has seen the previous chalk marks of a 'special' – perhaps to Blackpool which once saw hundreds of thousands of holiday makers arrive by train each summer.

With their best work long behind them by 1962, the 'Britannia' class fell into mixed traffic duties and freight work towards the end of their lives. No.70011 HOTSPUR, another Kingmoor engine, works south of Preston, near Farington, with an Up heavy mineral train in June 1964. Remember that these Pacifics were green beneath that grime.

(left) The overall appearance of rust prevails whilst the pipework beneath the cab has been covered in an orange coating.

(right) The smoke deflectors and pistons have received similar treatment although the red of the nameplate can surprisingly still be recognised. This location was one of my regular haunts as a child.

Class 4 No.75034, plus brakevan, rest at Skipton in May 1967. Having just arrived on the Carnforth allocation, the 4-6-0 was to be amongst the last of the BR Standards to work. Note the lining which would have remained to the end. Now, let's look at the weathering.

(right) The crest and lining on the tender sides are barely visible, although the rivet details are plain to see through the muck. It is keeping the detail visible which makes a weathered model look good.

(below) Water staining, all along the top of the smokebox and boiler, contrasts with the overall filthy condition of the engine. Notice the painted 'pretend' 10A shed plate which was tidier than many of the painted shed codes applied during this the last full year of UK steam.

A fairly clean BR Standard Class 4, No.80150, poses beneath the Tonbridge coal stage in June 1960. This Brighton based engine was already about half way through its life but after withdrawal, in October 1965, it was purchased for scrap by Woodham Bros., at Barry and we all know what happened to most of the steam locomotives which ended up there. The scale of weathering presented here is about as much as a lot of people could handle but the subtleness is certainly attainable, with care.

At first glance a very clean locomotive and, by comparison to some of the earlier illustrations it is. Even so, there is an accumulation of dust around the smokebox and a slight rusty stain around the base of the chimney.

(right) Further along and the cab door, roof and steps are a dull grubby colour compared to the tank sides, the cab hand rail knobs have a polished shine to them - Humbrol 27004 Gunmetal is excellent for reproducing this effect.

Stanier 8F No.48045, complete with a newly acquired Fowler tender (swapped for its Stanier tender during its recent 'shopping'), stands in Northwich shed yard during March 1959. These capable engines were used almost exclusively by 8E on the ICI hopper trains to and from Tunstead.

(left) Freight engines were rarely cleaned between works visits, and 48045 is, for now, in pretty good external condition, however the rust has formed around the wash-out plugs and accompanying surfaces.
(below) Already brake dust and rust are clearly present on the cylinders.

One of the ubiquitous 4F 0-6-0s, No.43840 with an LMS tender, stands outside the shed at Millhouses in March 1958.

Leaks and water stains along the boiler, note also the rust on the chimney

Rust and general 'crud' on the tender frames and springs

On the same day at 41C, resident 'Jubilee' No.45609 GILBERT AND ELLIS ISLANDS, with a Fowler type tender, also stands outside the shed taking in the spring sunshine. Considering this locomotive was an early casualty and had been withdrawn by September 1960, it was certainly acquiring the grime so often attributed to the 1960s level of cleanliness.

Rust around the cylinders and front steps.

(below) Light dusting on the tender sides obscuring part of the tender lining.

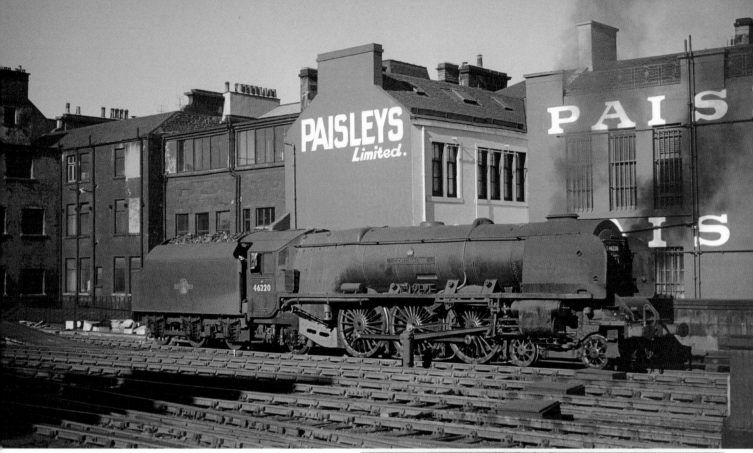

Green 8P No.46220 CORONATION backs down to Glasgow (Central) station to work a southbound express in July 1959. Cleaning standards were slipping, even for the top flight of BR's locomotive fleet.

(left) Heavy staining to the smoke deflectors with the original green livery unrecognisable, cylinders are showing signs of rust and brake dust.

(below) Rust forming around the boiler wash-out plugs and clinging to nooks and crannies around the cab front.

(above) Ex-CR 2F 'Beetlecrusher' tank No.56169 on shed at St Rollox, Glasgow in August 1959. This locomotive carries numerous levels of weathering.

(below) Dust and a little rust around the tank and cab area.

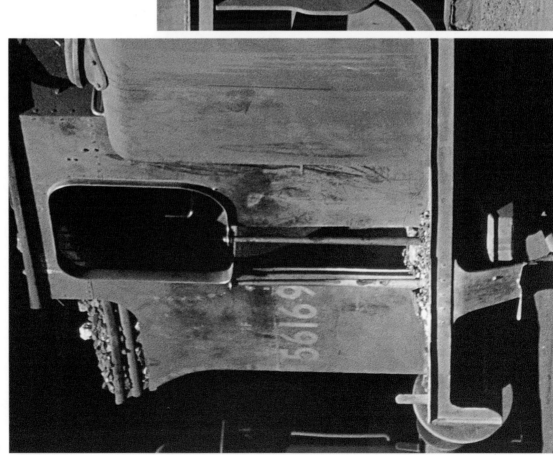

(below) Rust and old oil have given the cylinders and the motion a much worn appearance.

Ivatt Cl.4 No.43157 May 1961, fitted with a tablet catcher from its previous existence on the M&GN, rests on Retford GC shed in May 1961. Newly acquired from Boston, the 2-6-0 spent two years at Retford before moving on to Barrow Hill.

The cylinders are covered in a coat of all over grime which hides the original livery and on top of this there are signs of leaked oil and water.

(below) Leaking steam pipes have produced this off white staining.

(above) 8P No.46228 DUCHESS OF RUTLAND passes near Farmington on a Down parcels in July 1964. By now the Stanier Pacifics were running on borrowed time and nearly half the class had been withdrawn. Those still working were relegated to 'mixed traffic' duties such as this with the occasional express passenger working thrown in to cover for diesel failure. Of course, cleaning had fallen by the wayside even for these majestic beasts.

(right) Again cylinders covered in crud and leaked oil; a combination which has destroyed the original red livery completely.

(below) The red livery carried by this locomotive was now in a filthy state. Note the accumulated grime around the nameplate for instance.

The first Ivatt Class 2 2-6-0, No.46400, rests outside Millhouses shed in December 1959. Note that the tender is sporting a large new crest.

The smokebox door, boiler elements and cylinders all showing signs of rust.

Water leaks have mingled with the dust and streaked the boiler banding.

3F 0-6-0 No.47534 stables in the yard at Westhouses shed in June 1966. A stint working for the NCB at Williamsthorpe Colliery, by arrangement with BR, had given this 'Jinty' and a couple of its sisters, an extension of life. *(below)* Rust forming around the tank edges. *(right)* The rust has attacked the smokebox and chimney, areas that get very hot, and accumulated around the rivets.

23

4F No.43893, complete with tender cab, stands awaiting the next banking job at Manchester (Victoria) station in May 1964. Notice how weather has washed the dust over the entire locomotive. The solitary figure '4' on the cab side sheet, level with the Fireman's head, is of interest at this late date.

(left and below) The smokebox and chimney have suffered the same but in those areas the rust is beginning to come through the paint.

LMS built 4F, No.44278 adorned with a yellow stripe on the cab and also coupled to a tender cab. Condemned, during the previous January, the locomotive stands in the yard at Westhouses shed in June 1966 waiting for the tow which would take it to oblivion.

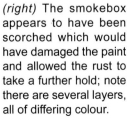

(left) A 4F that has seen better days, the rust has peeled the paint away from the metal and worked through all the accumulated grime.

(right) The smokebox appears to have been scorched which would have damaged the paint and allowed the rust to take a further hold; note there are several layers, all of differing colour.

Ex-LMS 3P No.41939 in store at Winsford & Over in July 1959 awaiting the inevitable. The LT&SR origins of this locomotive can be seen in the design.

Standing unused and unloved for a number of years, the rust has been allowed to spread out and continues to form around the tank tops.

The paint has been eaten away by the rust in places around the smoke box and chimney, note how orange coloured it is.

Stanier 8F No.48532 basks in the April sunshine at Buxton in 1967. Although the accumulated filth does not set this Stanier freight locomotive apart from others, the Darlington applied cabside numbers do. This was one of only a dozen or so 8Fs which received attention at North Road works in 1965.

(below) Covered in exactly two years worth of grime and filth since a Heavy General overhaul and repaint ensured an extended life to the end of BR steam. Notice how the wheels have collected layers of rust, brake dust and track dirt, but the axle boxes having been regularly oiled have survived the worst of it.

Dark orange rust on the cylinders contrasts with the overall warm grey colour of the main locomotive body. It is very easy to overdo this type of extreme weathering.

'Lord Nelson' No.30860 LORD HAWKE, on shed at Eastleigh in April 1960, still wearing the old emblem.

(left) The SR 4-6-0 was a green liveried locomotive, but you would be hard pushed to realise that was so beneath the grease and grime. Subtle shades here; note nowhere is really black (that colour combining grey, black, silver and unknowns, along with matt varnish is at work here) and there is a touch of rust on the steps. *(below)* The cab still has a touch of green under the layers of filth, contrast this to the colour of the tender. The locomotive's identity has been kept clean.

(above) N15 Nos.30456 SIR GALAHAD and 30800 SIR MELEAUS DE LILE stand together outside Basingstoke shed in March 1960. (right) Instantly recognisable as a Southern engine by its smoke deflectors, this green locomotive has picked up dust and grime around the lower parts of the boiler giving it a warm rusty brown glow. (below) The tender has also received a dusting from the thrown up combination of road dirt and brake dust leaving the lining just visible.

A work stained N class, No.31875, nears Worting Junction with a Down ballast train in September 1963. Note how dirty the top section of the tender side sheet is compared with the lower half; the dirt appears to be a continuation of that affecting the engine.

(below, left) Buffer beam grime clinging around the rivets and other exposed areas. The twin discs forming part of the head code looks stark by comparison.
(below, right) Smoke deflectors, firebox and boiler have all accumulated the orange brown dusting. Notice how the front of the deflector is clean compared to the rear half.

K class No.32347 on Brighton shed yard in April 1958. Still in steam, with a loaded tender, the 2-6-0 awaits its next turn of duty. No.32347 looks like a candidate for withdrawal but another five years in traffic would pass before that event took place.

(below) The rust on the tender is severe coupled with a slash on the cab side which was perhaps caused by impact damage? *(right)* Water staining under the boiler barrel completes the picture of an "unloved" specimen.

N15 No.30798 SIR HECTIMERE has its fire cleaned in the yard at Basingstoke shed in April 1960; by this time the class was a rare breed.

More rust around the boiler fittings on what is a relatively clean (if dusty) green locomotive.

Piston detail, showing the usual weathering highlights. Note the burning remnants of the fire being thrown out of the cab by the engineman (*main photo*).

S15 No.30838 rests in the sun at Basingstoke shed during September 1964.

(right) Pitted rust hides under the black paint of the smokebox door giving this engine a neglected and tired appearance.

(below) The well worn cab sides proudly display the locomotive number amongst the grime; the shiny patch above is perhaps due to the actions of the crew.

(top) Some four and a half years before the previous illustration, S15 No.30840 awaits its next turn of duty in the shed yard at Basingstoke in March 1960.

(above) Now to an unlined, black liveried locomotive. The motion looks well cared for and forms a contrast to the remainder of this engine.

(right) Cab side details include a little rust around rivets etc, the cab number is complete but the power classification has been nearly obliterated.

(top) U class No.31803 stands in the lines of locomotives outside Eastleigh shed in September 1964.

(above) In contrast to S15 No.30838 this lined black example displays vertical streaks on the tender sides, but the lining and crest are quite easily visible.

(left) The inevitable rust and dirt around the pistons has not yet obliterated the original lined black livery.

A1X No.32640 stands outside the London end of Eastleigh engine shed in June 1960.

(left) The rust has got hold of that wonderful tall chimney and the staining around the smokebox is plain to see.

(right) The tank sides still have the lining visible complete with a wet looking spillage along with a pair of lamps tucked into the side.

Auto-fitted Class H No.31520 rests in Tonbridge shed yard in June 1960.

(right) At its home depot, but with an incorrect shed plate, this engine has pitted and flaking rust around the smokebox, a touch of deep rust at the bottom of the door and what was once a white painted disc route indicator complete with duty number.

(below) The splasher lining is still intact, complete with two cleaner streaks and a clogged works plate with numerous coats of paint.

(above) E4 No.32506 outside Basingstoke shed in March 1960. This locomotive has the old emblem; the cab of clean N15 No.30798 is also visible. Besides the highlighted weathering details, note the coupling rod shows rust in the main but with small patches of oil stain. (left) With the lining virtually intact along the running plate and tank sides it maybe someone has given the engine a wash and brush-up in the recent past. However the staining along the smokebox and boiler depicts how quickly the outward appearance can deteriorate.

The tank sides clearly show how the dust has formed vertical streaks and created a dull coating over the gloss paint.

S15 30827 rests in Basingstoke shed yard in September 1963.

A smokebox door in a somewhat better condition. However, rust is just starting to show through on the top of the chimney.

(below) Streaking down the boiler, dust, rust and general wear and tear near the front cab section.

Push-pull fitted H class No.31177 stands at Dunton Green station in June 1960. Note the wrong-facing BR crest.

A locomotive of colour contrasts, the white/grey staining along the chimney gives a cold feel to the subject.

This continues along the boiler top and firebox and includes the long handled shovel on the tank top. Compare this to the warmer rust browns beneath the running plate and the deep black on the bunker side which has been given the "oily rag" treatment.

(above) 14XX No.1470 stands in Ashburton station dock on the branch auto-train in July 1957.

(below) A locomotive type synonymous with the GWR lines during steam days. Despite still remaining red the buffer beam has accumulated muck around the rivets. There is also a small pile of ash debris from the smokebox on the running plate,

(right) The dome has been coloured grey at first glance but closer inspection shows pitted rust underneath.

57XX No.3635 leaves Par on a Newquay bound local in June 1960.

The smokebox door is pitted with rust, the number plate discoloured, but someone has tried to clean some of the grime from the shed plate.

The carriages are clean but this locomotive is definitely not - grime and rust everywhere - even the lamp has seen better days.

43XX Mogul No.5311 stands outside Barmouth station awaiting an Up train in April 1957. The locomotive has been shopped in unlined green.

(below) A little dust has accumulated around the bottom of the smokebox area; however most of the black paint still remains untouched. *(right)* The front of the cylinder has begun to turn a deep orangey brown; a little weathering powder or dry brushing would easily replicate this.

In May 1961 14XX 0-4-2T No.1462 waits at Uffculme with the branch train to Hemyock. Note the ex Barry Railway composite coach which makes up the complete train.

A branch line engine depicting signs of care and attention, there is just a little dust at the back of the tank.

And the sand boxes also display dust and a faint coating of rust.

54XX class No.5410 on a Yeovil Junction to Yeovil Town auto-train on the four track stretch of line between the two locations in July 1963.

Another GWR mainstay and, despite being a humble tank engine (albeit specifically allocated to passenger duties), it was still painted green. The colour on the tank sides appears faded in comparison to the front portion.

The smokebox door and buffer beam have lost all semblance of colour and now appear to be virtually the same shade of warm grey.

'Hall' No.6940 DIDLINGTON HALL stands outside the former GWR shed at Exeter St Davids in May 1961.

(left) It seems that ex-GWR locomotives were generally kept in a cleaner condition than most, or was this just a rumour started by GWR fans? Looking at this particular engine you would have to agree, a little dust at the bottom of the smokebox but generally quite clean.

(below) Again a very thin film of dust below the boiler but overall the locomotive has obviously been "well groomed".

On the same day at Exeter, 'Castle' No.5020 TREMATON CASTLE rests in the yard.

Awaiting further duty this 'Castle' is in an overall clean condition complete with copper top chimney. However, a little dust has formed along the top of the boiler.

A dusty smokebox area but the lining on the boiler barrel and the wheel splashers is still very evident.

53XX No.6346 near Standish junction on a Gloucester to Swindon freight in May 1963.

In the last months of Western steam the neglect is all too apparent with rust and dust all over the cylinders and running plate,

Water staining and rust deposits all along the boiler. Compare this to the bright white of the lamp fixed on the buffer beam.

54XX Pannier No.5412 takes in the evening sun at Exeter engine shed in May 1961.

Unlined black in the sun light, this tank appears in good condition. Dust has collected around the grab handle on the tank side whilst the handle itself has worn shiny.

The dome exhibits subtle shades of brown and deep grey another task for the airbrush up close.

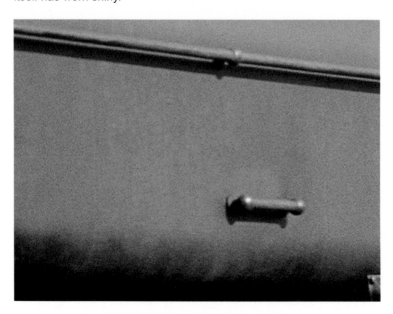

'Modified Hall' No.7913 LITTLE WYRLEY HALL pilots another of the class on a Down express near Craven Arms in June 1962.

Two 'Halls' are better than one, but both are filthy. The cab side number plate has lost its sheen and the tender lining and crest are just still visible.

Some of the rust colour appears to have been "washed away" on the piston of the front locomotive but still the green paint looks black.

On an evening in June 1960, 4575 class No.5515 runs light through Par en route to St Blazey shed.

(left) The grime has fought hard to obliterate the green paint but has not yet won. The number on the cab side still shows as its intended brass, albeit no longer polished.

(right) The subtle staining on the chimney and smokebox is easily missed at first glance; this is achievable with a good quality airbrush.

51XX class No.5198, working light engine to St Blazey shed around the curve at Par. This was Cornwall's only large 2-6-2T at the time when this photograph was taken in June 1960.

Ash and dust have combined with steam and water to produce this sludge on the boiler/smokebox area.

A little rust has formed over the cab window, notice the lining on the tank side is still visible and the red of the BR emblem is still bright.

(above) 45XX No.4559 near St Blazey shed in June 1960.

(lower right) The smokebox is the dirtiest part of this locomotive with the customary orange/brown staining. The back of the lamp on the running plate has seen better days but the shed plate still shows an 83 coding, part of the Newton Abbot/Plymouth division.

(below) Dusty and rusty here and there but generally looking "cared for". The handrail knobs on the cab have worn shiny with constant use.

Coming towards the end of its useful life, 'Manor' No.7819 HINTON MANOR smokes up with steam to spare outside Aberystwyth engine shed in August 1964.

(left) Although still green, the dirt is slowly accumulating over the whole locomotive whilst the copper top of the chimney is just visible. The light brown colouration of the smokebox mars the once black paint. *(below)* The smokebox door has been similarly defaced. The bare metal on the door handles stands out in contrast.

'Manor' No.7828 ODNEY MANOR stands in Aberystwyth shed yard, somewhat work-stained and rusty in August 1964!

Despite the overall external condition, the nameplate, number plate and tender sides are relatively clean.

The water stains have taken on a reddish tinge and would certainly stand out on a model, but could a GWR fan ever replicate this example?

Rubbing shoulders with the Southern Region residents, WR 'Grange' No.6879 OVERTON GRANGE takes water at Basingstoke's coal stage in September 1963.

(left) Another clean green engine. There is a little dust around the running plate but the lining on the cab side is still easily visible.

(below) More dust and ash has been deposited on the front running plate, however the buffer beam is still a bright red.

(top) J10 No.65134 stands in Northwich shed yard during August 1959.

(middle) A very work stained freight locomotive, still in steam but looking the worse for wear. The whole engine is a grimy grey/brown colour with leaks and rust all over the boiler.

(right) The tender fares no better with rusting springs and general filth obscuring the BR totem.

Stratford based J20 No.64689, ex-works 18th April, rests on March shed in early May 1958. Note the wrong-facing BR crest on the tender. For those wanting absolute accuracy, these are available through at least one source, and possibly more: The HMRS set of pressfix transfers (Sheet 14 – BR steam era, etc.) does contain two examples each of these, in both the large and small sizes. So, even the rivet counters are catered for now – to some degree. *(left)* Ex works, the tender is sporting just a little dust on the steps. Compare with the work stained example behind. For the record, No.64689 kept the wrong-facing crest to withdrawal. Others which were also 'blighted' were: Nos.64678, 64679, 64680, 64681, 64683, along with eight more (*see* also Yeadon's Register Vol.41). *(below)* Even though out from the shops for only a short time, the ash and steam have produced a dramatic effect on this otherwise clean locomotive; I wonder what the Running Foreman had to say about it!

K2 No.61771 lined out and with the old emblem, is still sporting a 40F plate. The 2-6-0 is brewing-up outside Darnall shed in October 1958.

The smokebox sports an untidy chalked reference to a recent or forthcoming working whilst the edges of the door appear shiny through the grime. *Humbrol's* metallic gunmetal would assist in achieving this finish.

Still with cab side and tender lining visible, the dusty ash has deposited a thin film on the top of the boiler, adjacent to the cab.

J11/3 No.64332 rests on the former GCR shed at Retford Thrumpton in November 1960.

(left) A quick glance shows a fairly clean locomotive but the water stains are apparent as is the usual layer of dust.

(below) On further inspection there is rust forming on the wheel splashers and around the heads of the rivets in this area, the dry brushing technique is ideal for representing this effect.

A3 No.60102 SIR FREDERICK BANBURY stands majestic outside the south shed at Grantham in May 1961.

(left) Express passenger locomotives, on the whole, were afforded an attempt to keep them clean and this photograph presents a relatively well kept example of a lined green type. However, spot the off-white leaks from the washout plugs.

(below) The buffer beams were cleaned in an attempt to keep the red warning panel on display. Despite this the dust and ash take there toll. Notice also the oily wheels on the pony truck.

(top) B1 No.61402, ex-Cowlairs, outside Eastfield shed in June 1959. This view shows the rounded Cowlairs footplate lining to full advantage.

(above) An ex-works locomotive, but look how quickly the grime and dust has accumulated. The brake dust has already formed a skin over the wheels, springs and the front of the cylinders.

(left) The boiler barrel has also accumulated a layer of dust and ash which is beginning to hide the shiny lined black finish, an ideal photograph for a light weathering project.

By now living on borrowed time, B17 No.61626 BRANCEPETH CASTLE rests in March shed yard during April 1959 awaiting its next turn.

The overall condition of the B17 appears to be good, but the layers of grime on the boiler are apparent.

Despite this the lining can still be seen on the running plate, splashers and the tender. The buffer beam is still a healthy red colour and the motion looks well oiled and cared for.

J72 No.69016 shunts stock south of York station in May 1959. Built in 1951, this tank locomotive was only eight years old when photographed by Keith Pirt.

(lower left) By 1963 most of the class had been withdrawn; the eight years of accumulated grime on No.69016 are clearly visible with rust formed around the running gear, and the paint missing from the top half of the chimney.
(below) The early BR emblem on the tank side and the number are clearly visible and has probably had the attention from an oily rag or two over the years.

J6 No.64188 poses on Retford Thrumpton shed in May 1959.

(above) Brake dust has been thrown up onto the running plate and the cab sides but the paintwork is still intact.

(right) Rust has begun to show around the smokebox rivets.

Gresley A4 No.60020 GUILLEMOT heads an Up Newcastle to Kings Cross express out of Peascliffe tunnel in clear sunshine during July 1959.

(below) One-time pride of the LNER, in BR days even the A4s were not exempt from the accumulated grime especially those allocated to Gateshead shed. The orange dust has clung to all the nooks and crannies on the streamlined casing. *(right)* The raked smokebox has borne the brunt of the high speed running and the once green paint has virtually disappeared under a mixture of dark grey grime, notice how the streaks have formed around the number plate.

A3 No.60107 ROYAL LANCER stands in the snow on the works reception lines at Doncaster shed in October 1962.

A relatively clean machine with the boiler bandings still visible. Note how the dust has been rubbed away on the smoke deflector near the handrail.

A classic case of orange rust on the cylinder casing and similar clean spots where depot fitters have worked.

Thompson L1 No.67774 rests up at Grantham shed in June 1961.

(below) The tank lining has been obliterated in small sections and rust has formed on the cab steps, has someone tried to clean the route availability indicator?

(below) Fully coaled and ready for its next turn of duty the grime on the L1 has formed streaky layers around the chimney and smokebox. The original overall black on the tanks has become that lifeless, matt finished grey/black which sometimes appeared to have a blue hue in there too.

(above) B1 No.61327 stands outside the rear of Canklow engine shed in March 1963.

(left) The smoke box 'burn' has resulted in the paint showing signs of rust around the shed plate, the white paint of which contrasts with the metallic finish of the number plate.

(right) The cylinders and smokebox are showings signs of rusting and staining, however the lining on the running plate is untouched.

(above) N2 No.69580, fitted with condensing apparatus, stands at the side of Grantham's south shed in June 1961.

(left) Grimy tank sides but the wrong-facing crest and lining are still visible with little signs of rust.

(left) There are signs of water staining around the smokebox, with cleaner areas around the rivets and condensing pipe.

(above) Peppercorn A1 No.60155 BORDERER at rest in the shed yard at York. The roller bearing fitted Pacific was photographed in June 1965.

(right) A relatively clean tender with the lining and crest clearly visible. The cab side has had a wipe over and what appears to be a bit of patch painting.

(below) The oil on the driving wheels compares in contrast to the dry effect on the pony truck front wheel.

D11 No.62661 GERARD POWYS DEWHURST in the yard at Gorton shed in October 1959.

(right) The chimney has taken some stick.

(bottom, left) Beneath the accumulated grime the engine number can still be read, thanks to the application of the "oily rag".

(bottom, right) Oil and grease have caked the works plate and the satin sheen stands out against the matt finish of the remainder of the 4-4-0.

Peppercorn K1 No.62060, in reasonable condition, stands in York shed yard in May 1965.

(left) Dirt prevails with rust coloured staining around the smokebox

(below) A heavy deposit of oil provides a wet look to the cylinder.

V2 No.60828 stands over the ash pits at York shed in April 1965.

(below) A grimy but well oiled engine at its home shed, the oil has changed the appearance of the colouration of the cylinders to a warm brown

Off-white stains remain along the boiler barrel where the locomotive remains un-cleaned; the smokebox however has had recent attention.

One of the vacuum fitted J72s, complete with train heating, No.68677 stands near Holgate Bridge, York in August 1959. A typical carriage pilot looked after by its crew.

A well-cared for tank engine in a famous location; a little dust has accumulated here and there, but look how clean the white lamps are.

Very clean tank sides with the number, route availability and BR crest all showing through, bright and clear. The dust has formed subtle shades of warm brown through to a colder grey.

Withdrawn O4/6 No.63913 stands outside the rebuilt former GC engine shed at Staveley in August 1963. This particular O4 was also a rebuild – from Class O5, whilst retaining the high cab.

(left) Rust staining from the boiler washout plugs contrast with overall grimy finish of the engine, notice the cleaner cab side number.

(below) Peeling paint and pitted rust around the chimney this photograph provides the basis for a withdrawn locomotive on your layout.

Tools & Materials

An airbrush, although not essential, is a great asset to have when weathering any kind of model. The smooth finish and misting effects that can be produced are hard to re-create in any other way. I have used various types including a basic *Badger*, and the more 'up-market' *Vivitar*, *Clarke*, *Premi-Air* and 'top-of-the-tree' *Iwata*. I have found that you really do get what you pay for. At the cheaper end of the range is the Badger which is fine for general scenic work. For a little more outlay, the *Clarke* and *Vivitar* machines are good, reasonably priced and produce a nice finish.

I would recommend either of these as a starting point as the price enables a reasonable entry point for the newcomer to learn the techniques and skill required to gain an acceptable end result. It is important to remember that a dual action brush, which is gravity fed, should always be the preferred option whatever the make and model.

For the more dedicated and experienced user, the *Iwata* range are the "bees-knees" both in terms of ease of use and the finished results that can be achieved. Although more expensive, it is well worth the superb finish it can create.

An Iwata Eclipse CS

The modelling magazine *British Railway Modelling* recently had a subscription offer of a *Premi-Air* G35 brush, which again is a very useful appliance.

One piece of equipment that is vital to the consistent finish of spray painting is a compressor. Aerosol cans of compressed air can be used, but are expensive and have a tendency to 'freeze up' at just the wrong moment. They are, perhaps, okay for the beginner, for a first attempt, but I feel many modellers from all aspects of the hobby may have been put off using an airbrush in the long term by their very use.

A Clarke Wiz Compressor

Aerosol cans of paint too have their uses, and especially come into their own as primers or undercoats. Easily obtainable, the ubiquitous *Halfords* range of primers and car paint are good for a first coat but, as with all aerosols, are difficult to control for any detailed work.

Compressors are available from various sources (listed on the penultimate page) and can range in price from approximately sixty-five pounds to several hundred. A moisture trap is another essential feature and if not available as a feature with the compressor of choice, they can be purchased separately and installed in-line before the air brush feed.

Weathering powders, washes and filters are all excellent tools for creating rust, dirt and other effects. The range available to the military modeller is very extensive and some of that particular range are very useful and should find a rightful place in the railway modeller's arsenal.

Mig, *Vallejo*, *Tamiya*, *Eazi-Products*, *Carrs* and *Green Scene* all produce excellent powders and pigments that are easily applied with a brush or applicator and in most cases are easily removed if the application has been over zealous at the first attempt.

Encompassing the varying but useful washes, filters, dyes and inks, *Modelmates* (formerly *Dirty Down*) recently introduced a range of aerosol cans of weathering dyes that are water soluble and are sprayed onto the subject and then removed to create the desired effect. The product is very good but difficult to apply to smaller scale items in this form, however I believe the content of the cans are soon to be made available separately for airbrush users in re-usable containers which should prove to be a useful medium.

Other washes, filters and effects are available from companies such as *Lifecolor*, *Com-Art*, *Tensocrom* and *Mig*, and although these are primarily aimed (no pun intended) at the military modeller, much of the range are particularly useful.

Finally. Please remember, unless a suitable air extraction system is available when you are spraying in the confines of a room/building etc., for your safety you should use a good quality face mask. For those able to house such things, an *Expo Tools* portable extraction paint booth should be considered.

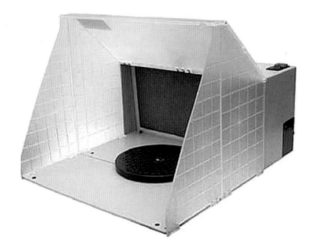

An Expo Tools Portable Extraction Booth

Stockists

The Airbrush Company *www.airbrushes.com* *01903 767800*
Iwata and *Premi-Air* products including airbrushes, compressors and spray booths, also *Com-Art* and *Tensocrom*.

Expo Tools *www.expotools.com* *01646 672440*
Vivitar, *Badger* tools and spares, also compressors, face masks, spray booths and a vast range of modelling products.

Netmerchants *www.netmerchants.co.uk* *0845 226 8266*
Mig, *Tensocrom*, *Tamiya*, *Vallejo*, *Lifecolor* products, also general paints and accessories.

Creative Models *www.creativemodels.co.uk* *01354 760022*
Mig, *Vallejo* products, plus paints and accessories

Squires *www.squirestools.com* *01243 842424*
Airbrush components and spares, face masks, *Tamiya*, *Carrs* weathering powders and a vast array of tools, paint etc.

Machine Mart *www.machinemart* *–stores nationwide*
Airbrushes, compressors and general airline accessories.

Modelmates *www.modelmates.co.uk* *07926 196471*
Weathering sprays and liquid.

Green Scene *www.green-scene.co.uk* *01905 24298*
Weathering powders and an extensive range of other scenic products.

Modeller's Mate *www.modellersmate.co.uk* *01728 720072*
Weathering powders, scenic accessories, airbrush spares, etc.

Finishing Touches *www.eaziproducts.com* *0116 2785134*
An extensive range of *Eazi* Weathering powders, *Vivitar* airbrush & weathering tools.

Although the above is not exhaustive, it is a listing of suppliers and their products I have used and found to be effective when weathering model locomotives and rolling stock.

Above all else, remember this is a hobby to be enjoyed. Experiment, but above all else, have fun doing so. I hope you have enjoyed the many beautiful and interesting photographs from Keith Pirt. Perhaps it has given you the inspiration to have a go at producing something original and distinctive amongst your locomotive fleet whatever era you model. On the following page is a more modern image which may well be the subject of a further title from Book Law Publications in the near future.

Please note I have no business connection with any of the above suppliers or manufacturers. My sole reason for listing is that of a satisfied customer.

END PIECE

Nearing the end of its operational life, 'Deltic' No.55013 THE BLACK WATCH is passing through Retford with a northbound express in April 1981.

(left) Perhaps aptly named THE BLACK WATCH, the yellow cab front appears to have been cleaned but the filth on the bonnet top has not – a regularly missed area for cleaning on diesel locomotives.

(below) The brake and road dust is masking the blue livery, notice also the fuel spillage splashes on the tanks.

LIKE THIS ONE?
CONTACT US IF YOU
WOULD LIKE TO SEE
AN ALBUM FEATURING
DIESEL TRACTION